YOUR KNOWLEDGE HAS VALUE

AF144629

- We will publish your bachelor's and
  master's thesis, essays and papers

- Your own eBook and book -
  sold worldwide in all relevant shops

- Earn money with each sale

Upload your text at www.GRIN.com
and publish for free

Bibliographic information published by the German National Library:

The German National Library lists this publication in the National Bibliography; detailed bibliographic data are available on the Internet at http://dnb.dnb.de .

Imprint:

Copyright © 2015 GRIN Verlag, Open Publishing GmbH
Print and binding: Books on Demand GmbH, Norderstedt Germany
ISBN: 978-3-668-11155-4

This book at GRIN:

http://www.grin.com/en/e-book/312311/agile-software-development-comparison-and-evaluation-of-existing-tools

Shah Niaz

Agile Software Development. Comparison and Evaluation of Existing Tools

GRIN Publishing

GRIN - Your knowledge has value

Since its foundation in 1998, GRIN has specialized in publishing academic texts by students, college teachers and other academics as e-book and printed book. The website www.grin.com is an ideal platform for presenting term papers, final papers, scientific essays, dissertations and specialist books.

Visit us on the internet:

http://www.grin.com/

http://www.facebook.com/grincom

http://www.twitter.com/grin_com

The Good, The Better and The Best

Shah Niaz Khan

Riphah International University

CONTENT

I. INTRODUCTION

Agile software development is a group of software development methods in which requirements and solutions evolve through collaboration between self-organizing, cross-functional teams. It promotes adaptive planning, evolutionary development, early delivery, continuous improvement and encourages rapid and flexible response to change. [1] In the agile software development different tools are used for the management of projects. Every one use these tools according to their need and requirements. if we take a look on the past then we came to know that different companies were mainly used MS Excel, word, and PowerPoint for storing and managing requirements and product backlogs and MS PowerPoint for managing projects. The development teams, on the other hand, used simple physical tools such as paper, sticky notes, and whiteboards. But it is experienced that the simple tools were insufficient for and unsupportive in managing large numbers of requirements and projects. So we got the need of some tools to manage and control all of the tasks in our project like scheduling, activities, planning, estimating, features, meetings, roles and release date etc.. Therefore a large number of tools are available in the market but the problem is to find the best one of them. Our task was to perform a detailed analysis of the agile tools, their usage and their needs on the basis of project work load. In this paper we present the result of our survey to find out a best agile project management tool to meet the company requirement and to support their needs. Therefore we have completed the survey on different tools practically like AgileZen, Rally, Versionone and some of others. This paper is organized as follows. Section 1 is based on the introduction of the problem and a brief knowledge of agile and agile tools. Section 2 is about the agile methodologies and of their usage. Section 3 is based on the detail note on existing agile tools and on their features. Section 4 is lists and describe the comparison of these tools on the basis of their features and usage which we have used in our survey. Section 5 is based on the evaluation criteria and on the detailed features of our chosen agile tool. Section 6 present the evaluation result of our own tool based on the criteria described in previous section. Section 7 describes the conclusion and observation and gives a brief result of this research.

II. AGILE METHODS

There has been a large number and a verity of agile methods available includes a specific technologies and practices of software development .Agile methods are based on iterative and evolutionary method [2][3]. Agile development   methods promote development, teamwork, collaboration and process adaptability throughout the life cycle of the project.The major methods are extreme programming, scrum, dynamic system development method [DSDM].Adaptive software development and feature driven development [FDD]. The Agile Manifesto represents the common principles and beliefs underlying these methods.However according to survey of agile methods by VersionOne Inc.

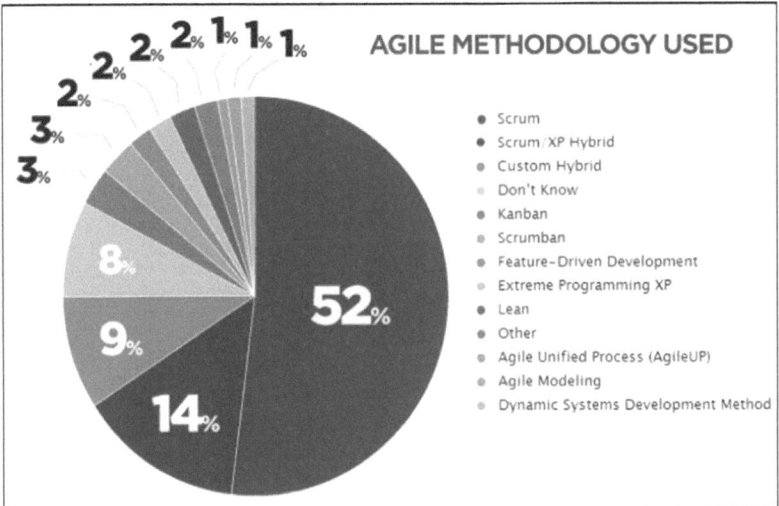

Figure 1: State of Agile Survey Results 2011 by VersionOne Inc.

[Source http://www.versionone.com][4]

Figure 1[4][5] shows the current usage of agile .Scrum is providing an agile for managing software projects and increasing of probability of success full development of software where XP focuses on the project level activities of implementing software .However both approaches are the way to success the principle of agile software development [5].

III. EXISTING TOOLS

There is a large number of agile tools are available in the market but according to our research and survey we have to select a few of them so we have select only six tools to perform the task and to   complete our survey . These are VersionOne, Jira, Rally, Microsoft TFS, AgileZen and Redmine.

A. *VersionOne*

VersionOne is an all in one agile project management platform that supports alignment between all three levels of enterprise agile project management [Portfolio, Program, and Team][6]. VersionOne is a very elegant and well structured tool to manage agile project management supporting today's leading edge development methods such as SCRUM, XP, Kanban, AgileUP and DSDM. . It's effective in terms of centralized management, simplified collaboration and effective project visibility[7].

Features:

- Collaboration
- Email Integration
- File Sharing
- Issue Management
- Milestone Tracking
- Percent-Complete Tracking
- Portfolio Management
- Project Planning
- Requirements Management
- Task Management [16]

B. *Jira*

JIRA [pronounced JEER-a] is Atlassian's project management software used by LDSTech for bug tracking, issue tracking, and task planning. LDSTech project teams use JIRA JIRA to organize and track various tasks in their projects.Jira is an excellent tool for a small team. For larger organizations and product development, Jira needs support of several plugins which integrate well with one another[8].

Features:

- Flexible Dashboards
- Direct Customer Involvement
- Agile, Scrum, Kanban
- Powerful Searching and Reporting
- Deployment Options
- Scalability and Workflow.[17]

C. Redmine

Redmine is a free and open source,[10] web-based project management and issue tracking tool. It handles multiple projects and subprojects. It features per project wikis and forums, time tracking, and flexible role based access control. It includes a calendar and Gantt charts to aid visual representation of projects and their deadlines. Redmine integrates with various version control systems and includes a repository browser and diff viewer[9]. Organizations that have plenty of different projects on the go can use Redmine to track issues, tickets, and time spent on each task. Redmine can also act as your company's central repository for documents and other project artifacts.

Features

- Multiple projects support
- Multiple subproject support
- Flexible role based access control
- Flexible issue tracking system
- Gantt chart and calendar
- Time tracking functionality
- Custom fields
- News, documents & files management
- Per project wiki and forums[18]

D. MicrosoftTFS

Team Foundation Server [commonly abbreviated to TFS] is a an agile software development tool by Microsoft which provides source code management[either via Team Foundation Version Control or Git], reporting, requirements management, project management, automated builds, lab management, testing and release management capabilities. It covers the entire Application Lifecycle Management. TFS can be used as a back end to numerous integrated development environments but is designed to provide the most benefit by serving as the back end to Microsoft Visual Studio or Eclipse [on Windows and non-Windows platforms].[11]

Features:

- Version control
- Work item tracking
- Project management functions
- Team build
- Data collection and reporting
- Team Project Porta
- Team Foundation Shared Services[19]

E. AgileZen

AgileZen is a simple, flexible, and cost-effective web-based software for project management built on ideas from agile, lean, and kanban methodologies. AgileZen provides agile project management applications to for software development. The company was acquired by Rally software in April 2010. AgileZen is a simple, visual, and collaborative way to manage your projects. Whether you're on a team or flying solo, AgileZen helps you stay organized.[12]

Features:

- Visualize your work
- AgileZen organizes your work visually, letting you see the big picture, while remaining focused on the task at hand.
- Communicate with your team
- AgileZen includes many ways to communicate the necessary information to your teammates.
- Get organized
- Avoid being overwhelmed and focus on the most important tasks at hand.
- Find ways to improve.[15]

F. Rally

Rally is an agile project management and portfolio management tools,The entire organization gains real-time visibility into the status of features and quality, priorities, roadblocks and risks.Rally provides release and iteration planning scheduling and tracking that supports your team's natural signaling. Rally helps you balance resources against your highest value features and build plans the whole team can commit to.[13]

Features:

- Project room makes collaborating easy.
- Real time picture of project status.
- co-ordinate multi-team releases so every feature and sub system stays synchronized with your commitments.
- Shared product backlogs, hierarchical projects, roll up reporting and advanced analytics.
- Integrated application lifecycle data provided to everyone.
- Idea Management, Agile portfolio management, time and Cost tracking, full quality management and development sandboxes.
- Rally Apps – extend Rally's functionality with customer features, displays and reports.[14]

IV. COMPARISON OF TOOLS

Organization uses an agile tool does not suggest that you will be successful with agile. Numerous applications offer tons of features that teams may never use yet your team(s) may be confused. Trying to leverage these features can consume valuable time causing confusion and distracting the team from the important work at hand.

Due to a large number of agile tools available in the market it is very hard to choose the best one of them to complete the project management activities. Our task has been performed to report a detail note on the comparison of these six agile development tools . This task was completed about comparison on the basis of their features and usage of the agile tools.

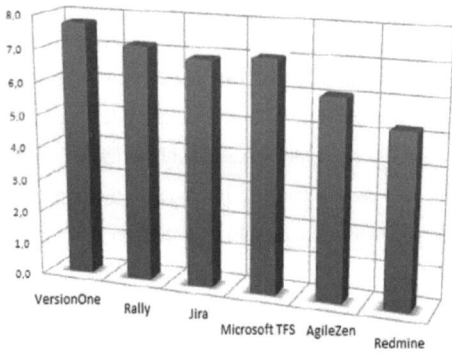

Figure 2 : Represent agile tools usage

For every company there is a tool for any agile project being worked on, but the key is to figure out which one is right for your organization. Hopefully this survey , based on some key attributes, will enable you to make the best choice. In summary, we have found that VersionOne and Rally provide the highest level of features for managing multiple agile projects and for established and mature teams. They offer the needed reporting mechanisms allowing business partners/clients to witness progress understand impediments and collaborate at a high level. Many teams today have remote resources and these tools are also equipped to allow offsite teamwork.[20] So what is important in selecting the appropriate tool for you? Many tools offer a free trial period that allows your team to understand the functionality and how to integrate within the organization.

Teams can take this opportunity to understand key features that are pertinent to what metrics and reporting may be critical to their needs. It also allows to see a full view of what they can expect while running an agile project by creating reports and planning stories.

TABLE I.: SUMMARY OF THE EVALUATED TOOLS

Features	Tools					
	Version one	TFS	Rally	Jira	Redmine	Agilezen
Build For Agile						
Visual product roadmap	✓	×	✓	×	✓	✓
Goal planning	✓	×	×	×	✓	✓
Costumer idea management	✓	×	✓	✓	×	✓
Retrospective management	✓	×	×	×		
Time tracking	Partial	✓	✓	partial	✓	partial
Scalability						
Programming- level planning and reporting	✓	✓	✓	×	×	×
Cross-project teams	✓	✓	×	×	✓	✓
Project and role based security	✓	✓	Partial	✓	×	partial
Customer reporting and visualization						
Basic agile reporting (velocity, burn down)	✓	✓	✓	✓	✓	✓
Safe metrics and support	✓	×	✓	×	×	×
Epics bubble chart, relationship ,dependency diagram, heat map	✓	×	×	×	×	×
Epics time line	✓	×	✓	×	✓	×
Deployment and step						
Web based UI	✓	✓	✓	✓	✓	✓
Support multiple agile methodologies	✓	✓	✓	✓	✓	✓
Customizable terminology	✓	×	×	×	×	partial
Technology						
Open, web-services API	✓	✓	Partial	✓	✓	✓
Open integration platform	✓	✓	×	✓	✓	✓
.NET and Java SDK	✓	✓	Partial	×	×	✓

10

V.   EVALUATION CRITERIA

We have select the VersionOne as the best tool among all the agile development tools on the basis of their features and usage as it is used by a large number of organizations and teams. We have followed the twenty-one criteria[21] that were used for evaluating the tool. This criteria is :

Extensibility referring to whether the tool can be modified or extended. Here, we evaluated whether a tool provided access to the source code, and whether it was offered on a commercial or open source license.

• **Usability** concerning the general usability of the tool. Here, we rated the tools solely for their ease of use, also taking into account whether it was necessary to study tool documentation and tutorials.

• **Connectivity** describing the connectors, or plug-ins, provided by the tool vendors such as Integrated Development Environments (IDEs), bug-tracking systems or traditional project management tools. Here, we evaluated the availability of such connectors; we also took into account both their number and variety.

• **Searching** referring to the searching capabilities of the tool. Here, we evaluated the availability of searching options, taking into account the searching factors.

• **Grouping** standing for the capability to group items in a product backlog. We evaluated whether the tool enabled grouping of product backlog items.

• **Simultaneous editing** implying whether multiple users could simultaneously edit the same artifact in the tool. While this might seem a basic requirement for tools, we still consider it mainly due to the absence of such options in basic tools such as spreadsheets used for storing backlogs.

• **Story status tracking** referring to the opportunity to track the status of a user story. Here, we evaluated whether the tool allowed to record progress of the story. The status could simply be represented as a string,

• **Group status tracking** enabling grouping of product backlog items. We evaluated whether it was possible to track the status of the group.

• **Overall status tracking** referring to the options of viewing the overall project status. This could imply a highlevel summary view of the Sprint backlogs, or a chart showing the number of completed product backlog items over time. For this criterion, we evaluated whether the tool provided feedback on project status and what kind of status reports it generated.

• **Sorting/Filtering** standing for the sorting and filtering options. Here, we evaluated whether the tool provided sorting and filtering services and whether it could sort by several criteria and filter by typing in keywords.

• **Sprint backlog** dealing with the ability to create and manage a Sprint backlog. Here, we evaluated whether it was possible to prioritize and order Sprint backlog items.

• **Estimation** concerning the estimation ability of user stories and tasks. For this criterion, we evaluated whether it was possible to enter estimations of user stories and tasks, and how flexible the estimation measures were.

• **Stories.** Here, we evaluated the options offered for creating and describing user stories. Specifically, we evaluated whether it was possible to group stories into epics.

• **Tasks** referring to the tasks required for implementing a user story. We evaluated whether it was possible to break down user stories into smaller tasks in a Sprint backlog.

• **Testing.** Here, we evaluated the support for testing tasks. This could be realized in form of connectors to testing tools or by enabling the creation of special testing tasks.

• **Teams** referring to team management. For this criterion, we evaluated whether it was possible to create teams within the tool, assign team members, and make changes to the team capacity over time.

• **Planning** covering the ability to support Sprint planning, that is, selecting items from the product backlog and entering them in a new Sprint. We evaluated whether this was possible, and whether the capacity of the created Sprint was automatically matched to the team assigned to that Sprint.

• **Progress** referring to the status of the story or task on a greater level of detail. Here, we evaluated whether the tool enabled entering the amount of work performed on a story or task, and whether it was also possible to see how much work remained.

• **Board** covering the provision of a virtual task board for storing user stories and tasks. Here, we evaluated the availability of a task board, and, if so, whether it was interactive and whether it was possible to drag and drop tasks and user stories on the board.

• **Burndown** describing whether the tool included Sprint burndown charts, whether they were updatable, and how visually clear they were.

• **Remote workplace** relating to the opportunity to access a tool remotely. Most often, this implies that a tool needs to be deployed as a web application so that the user can access the application even outside the office network.

VI. EVALUATION RESULT

As a result of our evaluation, we discovered that all the evaluated tools focused on team-level rather than management-level aspects.[21] The tools included features such as advanced virtual task boards for facilitating development within the teams, but provided only rudimentary requirements and project management support. Moreover, tools covering more features were complicated to use.

The results of our tool evaluation are summarized in Figure 2 and Table 1. The evaluation had led us to a number of conclusions. First, we noticed that the tools were targeted towards Scrum Masters and development teams rather than managers. Some tools studied provided virtual task boards, as well as possibilities to break down user stories into more detailed tasks and functions for storing and managing the tasks.

The second, more important conclusion concerned the usability of the tools studied. Tools with higher usability offered less features, and tools which provided many features had a notably lower usability.

VI. CONCLUSION

Despite the growing availability and complexity of agile tools, there is lack of tool selection guidelines and case studies. In this paper, we have attempted to shed some light on the matter by presenting the results of a case study of agile tools. As part of our research, we performed an

evaluation of six agile tools available on the market using a detailed list of evaluation criteria. During our attempt to select an adequate tool , we found out that the tool evaluation criteria,[21] though well defined, proved to be insufficient for specifying the company's needs.Therefore we rate VersionOne the highest among the tools reviewed. Microsoft TFS,Rally and JIRA fall in Costumer idea management, Retrospective management, Epics bubble chart, relationship ,dependency diagram, heat map. Redmine and agilezen also missing too many key features and its development status is uncertain, so we don‚Äôt recommend it. However, each organization should consider its own situation and feature needs before choosing a tool. Particular features may be very important for one organization but not for another.

VII. REFERENCES

[1] Agile software development, Wikipedia [online]
available:
http://en.wikipedia.org/wiki/Agile_software_development
[retrieved: December, 2014].

[2] Software Development: Iterative & Evolutionary [online]
available:
http://www.informit.com/articles/article.aspx?p=102256
[retrieved: December, 2014].

[3] C. Larman, Agile and Iterative Development: [Book]
A Manager's Guide. Boston: Addison Wesley, 2004.
[online]
available:
http://www.abebooks.com/Agile-Iterative-Development-Managers-Guide-Larman/9853250143/bd
[retrieved: December, 2014].

[4] State of Agile Development Survey Results [online] available:
http://www.versionone.com/state_of_agile_development_survey/2011/
[retrieved: December, 2014].

[5] Comparative Study on Agile software development methodologies [online] [paper]
available: http://arxiv.org/ftp/arxiv/papers/1307/1307.3356.pdf
[retrieved: December, 2014].

[6] VersionOne [Agile Development Tool] [online]
available:
http://www.versionone.com/

[retrieved: December, 2014].

[7] Comprehensive agile project management tool [online]
available:
http://www.softwaretestingclass.com/70-comprehensive-agile-project-management-tools-list/
[retrieved: December, 2014].

[8] Beginner's_guide_to_JIRA, Web [online]
available:
https://tech.lds.org/wiki/Beginner's_guide_to_JIRA
[retrieved: January, 2015].

[9] Redmine, Wikipedia [online]
available:
http://en.wikipedia.org/wiki/Redmine
[retrieved: January, 2015].

[10] Redmine, Web [online]
available:

http://www.redmine.org/
[retrieved: January, 2015].

[11] Microsoft TFS, Wikipedia [online]
available:
http://en.wikipedia.org/wiki/Team_Foundation_Server
[retrieved: January, 2015].

[12] AgileZen, Web [online]
available:
http://www.agilezen.com/
[retrieved: January, 2015].

[13] Rally the Agile tool, Web [online]
available:
https://www.rallydev.com/about/what-is-rally
[retrieved: January, 2015].

[14] Features of Rally, Web [online]
available:
http://agiletools.info/rally/
[retrieved: January, 2015].

[15] Features of AgileZen, Web [online]
available:
http://www.agilezen.com/
[retrieved: January, 2015].

[16] Features of VersionOne, Web [online]
available:
http://www.capterra.com/project-management-software/spotlight/101338/VersionOne/VersionOne
[retrieved: January, 2015]

[17] Features of Jira, Web [online]
available:
https://tech.lds.org/wiki/Beginner's_guide_to_JIRA
[retrieved: January, 2015]..

[18] Features of Redmine, Web [online]
available:
http://www.redmine.org/projects/redmine/wiki/Features
[retrieved: January, 2015]..

[19] Features of Microsoft TFS, Web [online]
available:
http://msdn.microsoft.com/en-us/library/ms364062%28v=vs.80%29.aspx
[retrieved: January, 2015]..

[20] A comparative look at top agile tools, Web [online]
available:
http://www.captechconsulting.com/blog/kevin-erickson/comparative-look-top-agile-tools
[retrieved: January, 2015]..

[21] Comparative Study on Agile software development methodologies [online] [paper]
available: http://arxiv.org/ftp/arxiv/papers/1307/1307.3356.pdf
[retrieved: January, 2015].